STRUGGLE FOR SURVIVAL

SURVIVAL

FLORIDA PANTHER COMEBACK

BY TIM COOKE
ILLUSTRATED BY ALESSANDRO VALDRIGHI

BEARPORT
PUBLISHING

Minneapolis, Minnesota

Credits: 20, © Jo Crebbin/Shutterstock; 21, © Steven Blandin/Shutterstock; 22t, © Danita Delimont/ Shutterstock; 22b, © Andreas Rose/Shutterstock.

Editor: Sarah Eason
Proofreader: Harriet McGregor
Designers: Jessica Moon and Steve Mead
Picture Researcher: Rachel Blount

DISCLAIMER: This graphic story is a dramatization based on true events. It is intended to give the reader a sense of the narrative rather than a presentation of actual details as they occurred.

Library of Congress Cataloging-in-Publication Data

Names: Cooke, Tim (Tim A.) author. | Valdrighi, Alessandro, illustrator.
Title: Struggle for survival : Florida panther comeback / by Tim Cooke ;
  illustrated by Alessandro Valdrighi.
Description: Bear claw books. | Minneapolis, Minnesota : Bearport
  Publishing Company, [2022] | Series: Saving animals from the brink |
  Includes bibliographical references and index.
Identifiers: LCCN 2021002694 (print) | LCCN 2021002695 (ebook) | ISBN
  9781636910499 (library binding) | ISBN 9781636910567 (paperback) | ISBN
  9781636910635 (ebook)
Subjects: LCSH: Florida panther--Juvenile literature. | Endangered
  species--Florida--Juvenile literature.
Classification: LCC QL737.C23 C6726 2022 (print) | LCC QL737.C23 (ebook)
  | DDC 599.75/2409759--dc23
LC record available at https://lccn.loc.gov/2021002694
LC ebook record available at https://lccn.loc.gov/2021002695

For more information, write to Bearport Publishing, 5357 Penn Avenue South, Minneapolis, MN 55419. Printed in the United States of America.

CONTENTS

CHAPTER 1
PANTHERS IN DANGER

In the 1800s, Florida panthers lived throughout the southeastern United States.

Many people hunted the animals out of fear and to protect their **livestock**.

As people built roads and houses, the size of the panthers' **habitat** got smaller, and their **population** shrank.

By the mid-1900s, there were very few of the animals left. They were now found only in a small part of southwestern Florida.

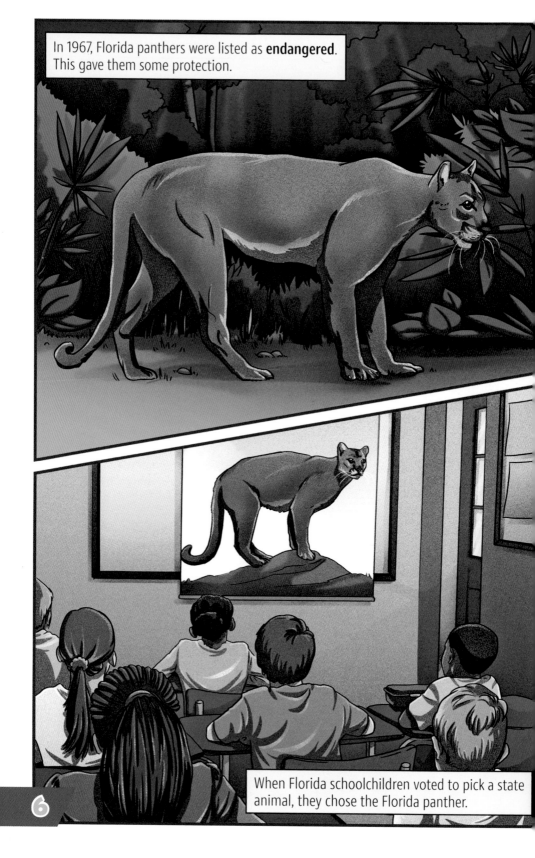

In 1967, Florida panthers were listed as **endangered**. This gave them some protection.

When Florida schoolchildren voted to pick a state animal, they chose the Florida panther.

CHAPTER 2

A BOLD EXPERIMENT

In 1989, a **refuge** was created to provide a safe place for the panthers to live. But would this be enough to save the animals?

Florida Panther

NATIONAL WILDLIFE REFUGE

Biologist Mark Lotz who studied the Florida panthers wanted to find out.

GOOD JOB CATCHING THIS PANTHER, EVERYONE.

YES! IT IS THE EST WAY TO CHECK F THE POPULATION IS HEALTHY.

THAT PATCH OF HAIR IS GROWING STRANGELY. ALL THE PANTHERS WE HAVE SEEN SHOW THE SAME SIGNS OF **INBREEDING**.

THIS PANTHER HAS THE SAME **KINK** IN THE TAIL, TOO.

INBREEDING IS GOING TO AFFECT THEIR HEALTH. WE HAVE TO FIND OUT MORE.

LET'S GET A **RADIO COLLAR** ON HIM.

Mark and his fellow scientists tracked the panthers.

WHAT ARE WE GOING TO DO?

They discovered that many of the animals were unhealthy. Some were born with heart problems, and others were unable to have babies.

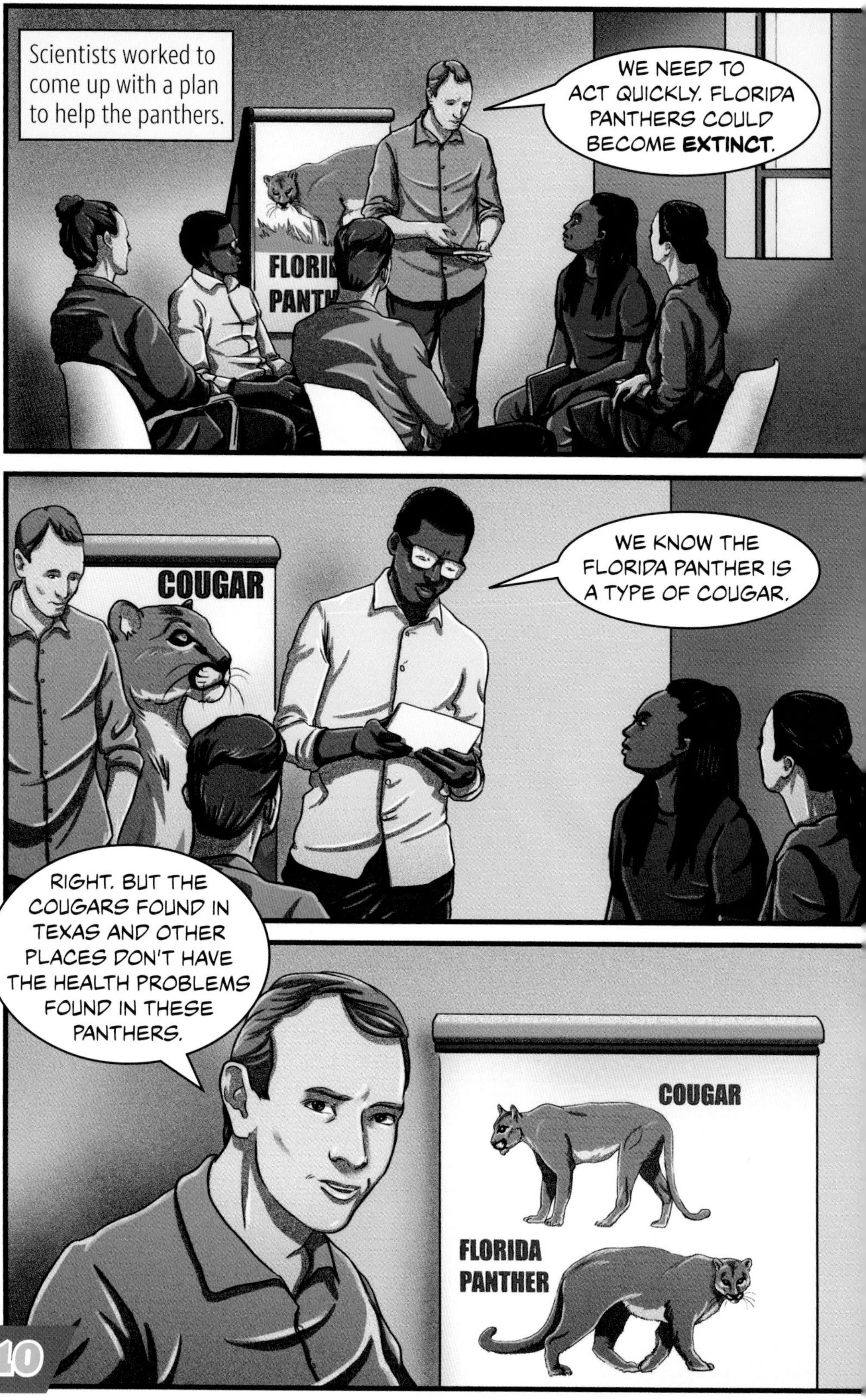
Scientists worked to come up with a plan to help the panthers.
WE NEED TO ACT QUICKLY. FLORIDA PANTHERS COULD BECOME **EXTINCT**.
COUGAR
WE KNOW THE FLORIDA PANTHER IS A TYPE OF COUGAR.
RIGHT. BUT THE COUGARS FOUND IN TEXAS AND OTHER PLACES DON'T HAVE THE HEALTH PROBLEMS FOUND IN THESE PANTHERS.
COUGAR
FLORIDA PANTHER

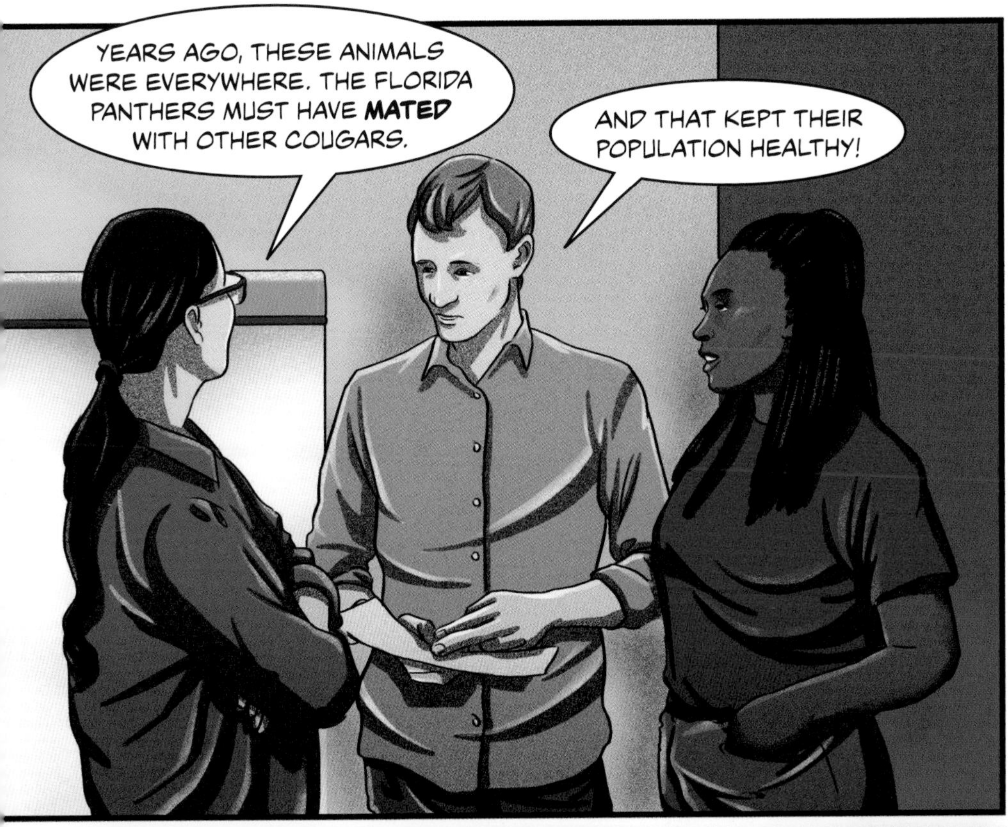
YEARS AGO, THESE ANIMALS WERE EVERYWHERE. THE FLORIDA PANTHERS MUST HAVE **MATED** WITH OTHER COUGARS.
AND THAT KEPT THEIR POPULATION HEALTHY!

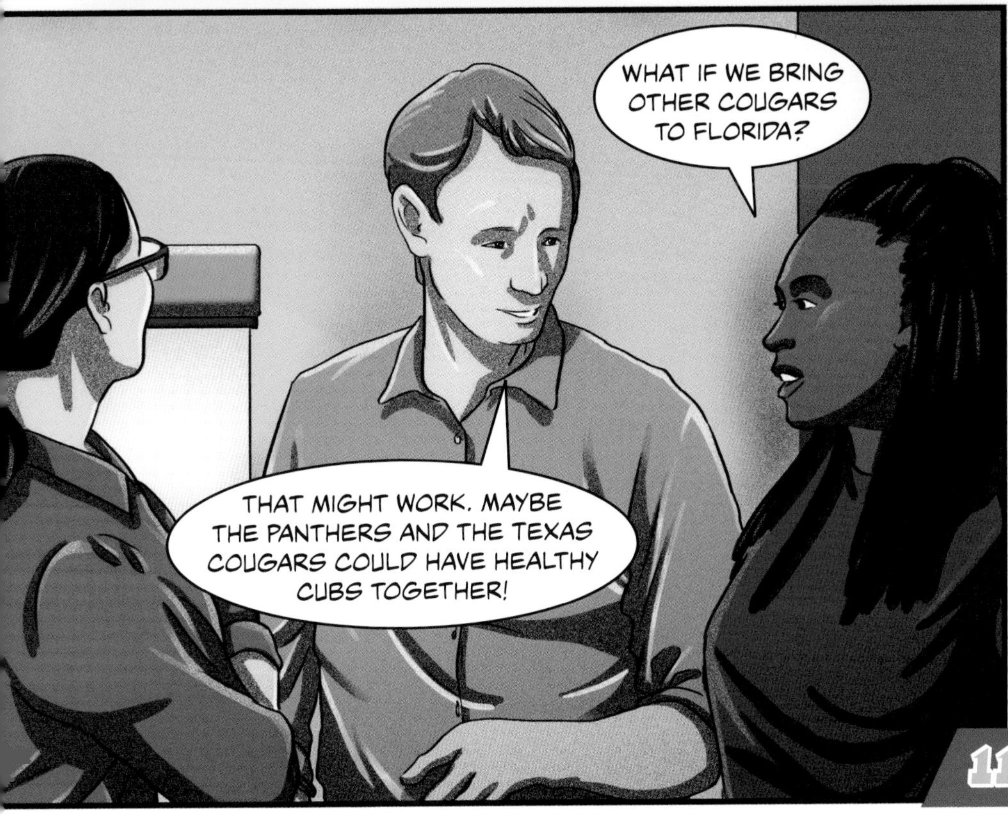
WHAT IF WE BRING OTHER COUGARS TO FLORIDA?
THAT MIGHT WORK. MAYBE THE PANTHERS AND THE TEXAS COUGARS COULD HAVE HEALTHY CUBS TOGETHER!

The scientists put their plan into action.

It was difficult to catch the cougars. Like Florida panthers, these animals usually have large **territories**.

They can also run very quickly.

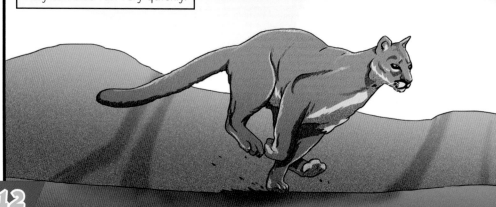

But scientists were finally able to catch eight females. They used special drugs to make them sleep. Then, the cougars were carefully placed in cages.

Soon, the cougars from Texas were safely moved to Florida.

The animals were released into the Florida wilderness.

THEY'RE BEAUTIFUL!

LOOK HOW SILENTLY THEY MOVE!

NOW WE HAVE TO WAIT TO SEE IF THE PLAN WILL WORK.

The scientists had many questions. Would the cougars be able to survive in Florida's **climate**?

Would people, or perhaps even the Florida panthers, kill the new animals?

And, most importantly, would the Florida panthers and the cougars from Texas be able to have healthy babies together?

CHAPTER 3
THE FLORIDA PANTHER'S FUTURE

In 1996, Mark and the other scientists discovered that the Florida panthers and the cougars had mated—and the kittens were healthy!

The scientists had taken a big step toward helping the panthers.

The number of healthy animals slowly increased.

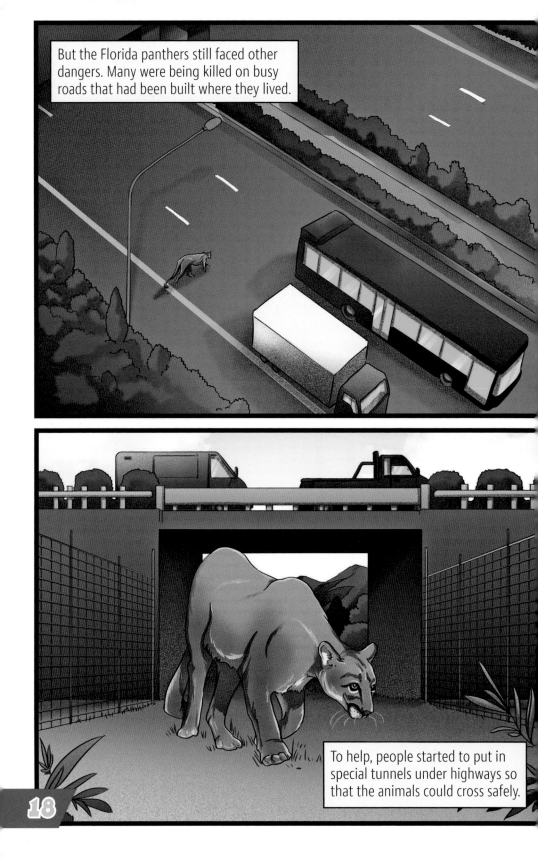

But the Florida panthers still faced other dangers. Many were being killed on busy roads that had been built where they lived.

To help, people started to put in special tunnels under highways so that the animals could cross safely.

Today, around 130 panthers live in the Florida wilderness. Thanks to the efforts of Mark Lotz and others, these amazing animals were saved from the brink.

FLORIDA PANTHER FACTS

In 1973, Congress passed the Endangered Species Act. This law protects animals and plants that are in danger of dying out. Activities such as hunting, capturing, harming, or collecting endangered species are illegal under this law.

The Florida panther was one of the first species listed under the Endangered Species Act. They are still on the list today.

FLORIDA PANTHERS CAN GROW TO ABOUT 7 FEET (2 M) LONG AND ABOUT 2.5 FT (0.8 M) TALL.

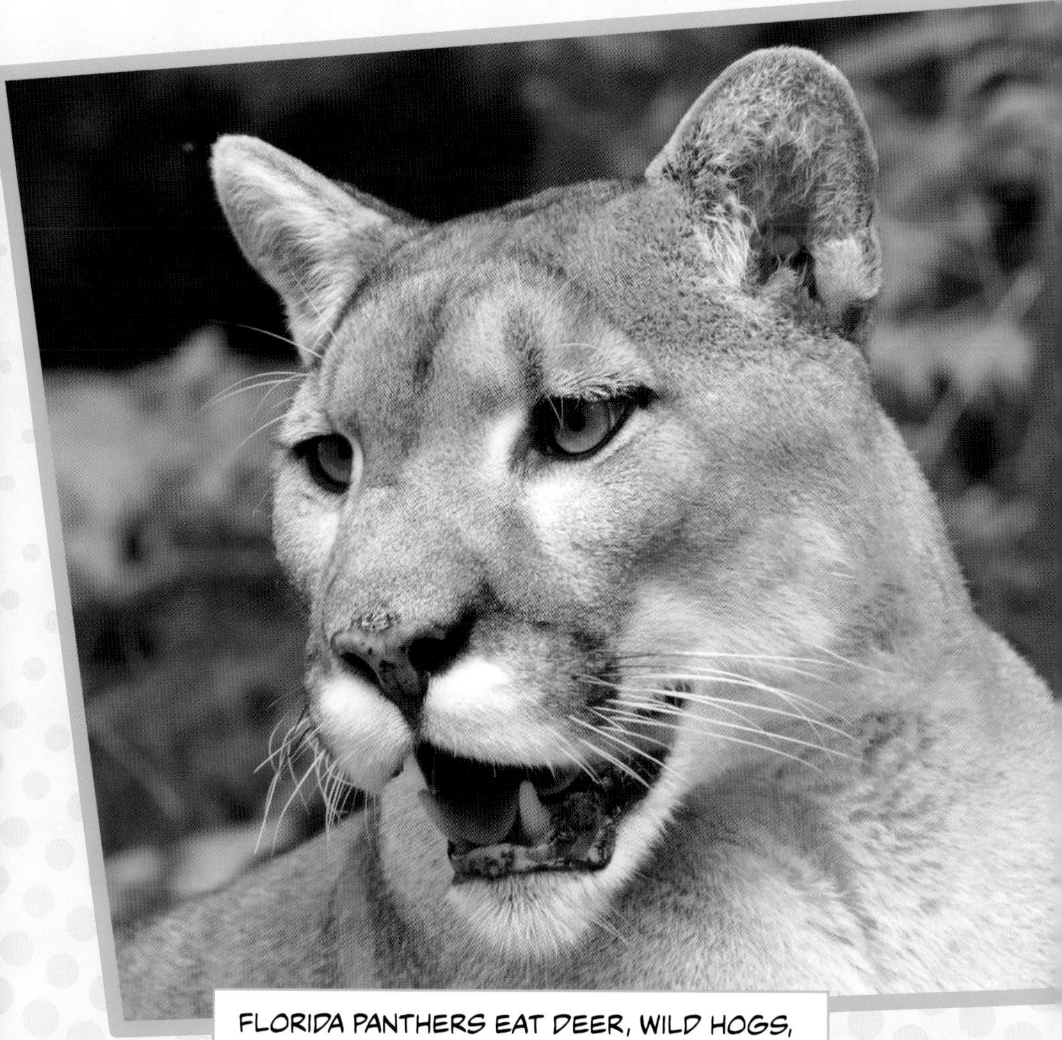

FLORIDA PANTHERS EAT DEER, WILD HOGS, ARMADILLOS, RACCOONS, AND SOME BIRDS.

Before 1800, the number of Florida panthers living in Florida was estimated to be 1,360. Today, there are thought to be around just 130 of the big cats.

OTHER CATS IN DANGER

The Florida panther is one type of cat that is making a comeback. Other members of the cat family are also struggling.

TEXAS OCELOT

There are only around 80 to 120 Texas ocelots living in Texas today. The cats are **threatened** by the loss of their natural habitat. They are often hit by vehicles on the highway.

TEXAS OCELOTS ALSO HAVE MANY HEALTH PROBLEMS CAUSED BY INBREEDING.

SNOW LEOPARD

Snow leopards live in eastern Asia. Today, there are an estimated 2,700 to 3,300 snow leopards left in the wild. They are threatened because they do not have enough **prey**. These large cats are also hunted by people.

PEOPLE HUNT SNOW LEOPARDS FOR THEIR FUR.

GLOSSARY

biologist a scientist who studies plants or animals

climate the typical weather in a place

endangered in danger of dying out

extinct died out

habitat where a plant or animal normally lives

inbreeding the mating of closely related individuals; inbreeding often makes a population unhealthy

kink a sharp twist or curve in something straight

livestock farm animals

mated came together to produce young

population the total number of a kind of animal living in a place

prey animals that are hunted or caught for food

radio collar a collar that transmits radio signals and is fitted to an animal to help people monitor the animal

refuge a place that provides shelter or protection

territories areas of land where an animal lives

threatened to be in danger of dying out

INDEX

READ MORE

Adamson, Thomas K. *Mountain Lion vs. Coyote (Animal Battles)*. Minneapolis: Bellwether Media, 2021.

O'Daly, Anne. *Big Cats (Animal Detectives)*. Tuscon, AZ: Brown Bear Books, 2020.

Tomljanovic, Tatiana. *Cougar (Backyard Animals)*. New York: AV2, 2019.

LEARN MORE ONLINE

1. Go to **www.factsurfer.com**

2. Enter "**Panther Comeback**" into the search box.

3. Click on the cover of this book to see a list of websites.